If I were a Tree

By Anita Kay Lasanowski

AuthorHouse™
1663 Liberty Drive
Bloomington, IN 47403
www.authorhouse.com
Phone: 1-800-839-8640

First published by AuthorHouse 06/09/2011

ISBN: 978-1-4634-1280-7 (sc)

Printed in the United States of America

Any people depicted in stock imagery provided by Thinkstock are models,
and such images are being used for illustrative purposes only.
Certain stock imagery © Thinkstock.

This book is printed on acid-free paper.

This book is dedicated to

my grandchildren,
my nieces
and
my nephews.

If I were
a tree
all would look up
at me.

I would grow

high
up into
the
sky.

I would play
with nature
and do magic
with the wind.

I could make my
leaves dance in
the breeze,
turn their colors and
make them fall to the ground.

After a winter's
blanket of snow
I could make
new leaves grow.

I could stretch my
branches far and wide.
Homes and shelter I'd provide.
I'd take them in each and all
creatures seen
and those too small.

A tree
towering high
above
the
rest
you could be assured
I'd do
my best.

I would make the
air sweet
and better to breathe.
All would benefit
from the likes of me.

So if you would
like to
but just can't be
grab a shovel
and plant a tree.

Just for fun

Which of the following can you find in a tree?
1. Banana
2. Monkey
3. Raccoon
4. Apple
5. Woodpecker
6. Pineapple

Which of the following is not a type of tree?
1. Tulip tree
2. Weeping willow tree
3. Pine tree
4. Lilac tree

Which of the following can you make from a tree?
1. Pencil
2. Toothpick
3. Rocking chair
4. Boat

Answers

Which of the following can you find in a tree?

- All but pineapples, they grow in the ground.

Which of the following is not a type of tree?

- A lilac is not a tree it's a bush

Which of the following can you make from a tree?

- All of them

Author Biography

Anita has always had a concern for the preservation of nature. She has integrated her interest through instruction as a Girl Scout leader. As a scout leader in Northern Indiana she initiated community events involving programs designed to educate as well as give back to the community.

About the Book

"If I were a tree" enables nature lovers to imagine life as a tree. As you read you may realize the significance that a tree contributes to the environment. You may just be inspired to promote others to take action and share your love for nature.

Grand daughter Lilyonna with daughter Hollie

www.ingramcontent.com/pod-product-compliance
Lightning Source LLC
Chambersburg PA
CBHW060828290526
45792CB00005BB/1842